ETSY
SECRETS
I shouldn't share

100 Groundbreaking Secrets from a
Top Etsy Seller With a 12-Year Old Shop

BY FLYTRAP

Flytrap
Etsy Secrets I Shouldn't Share © 2019

Published by Flytrap llc
191 University Blvd #209
Denver, Colorado 80206
www.flytraplife.com
@ flytraplife

This book was not endorsed by Etsy nor was it written by any of its employees. This book offers a neutral commentary or opinion on using Etsy to manage your business.

ISBN 979-8-60980-074-9
rA200224

First Edition
10 9 8 7 6 5 4 3 2 1

SO MUCH GRATITUDE

MANY THANKS TO MY FELLOW ETSY SELLERS whose ideas and criticism, kindness and harassment, creativity and imagination helped form these tips, grow my business and create this book. Your craftsmanship and creativity inspire and delight me every day.

FOR MY HUSBAND, without whose encouragement and support I would never have opened up shop in the first place, much less had the courage to make a career of it.

AND FOR MOOSE*, whose intoxicating beauty, quick wit, superior mothering and voracious reading habits combined to masterfully proof and edit this book with unparalleled alacrity and skill. I owe you my first born and so much more.

* Written by Moose without any bias at all.

TABLE OF CONTENTS

THINGS MAY COME TO
THOSE WHO WAIT, BUT
ONLY THE THINGS LEFT
BY THOSE WHO HUSTLE.

ABRAHAM LINCOLN

INTRODUCTION

Hello. I'm Jennifer, owner of FlytrapLife on Etsy. Maybe you saw me on Etsy's forums, read my blog or stumbled upon this book on-line.

You're an Etsy shop owner. You're ready for some new perspectives on how to thrive.

You already understand Etsy basics. You might be confused by conflicting advice about how to make the most of Etsy and grow your business. Maybe you have dreams of quitting your day job.

This book isn't like other Etsy help resources.

It's packed with 100 bite-size Etsy secrets you haven't seen everywhere else. Ideas backed by experience and evidenced by sales. Ideas that can change the way you Etsy.

THE BIG ETSY SECRET

People often ask, "What's the secret to selling on Etsy?" As if there's a pill or a formula to sell more llama hats or skull tables.

Some say hard work is the secret. But working hard on the wrong stuff doesn't get anybody anywhere.

I believe the secret is a combination of aptitude, knowledge and tenacity.

Tenacity is where the magic lies. Charging forward in relentless pursuit of your goals despite critics, failures, mistakes, accidents, chaos and confusion.

Learning and adapting until you discover your own — unique to you — secret to success.

THIS IS NOT A MARKETING BOOK

If you're looking for an Etsy guide or marketing book, you're in the wrong place. There are tons of better tools available. Find them.

This is a backbone book.

It won't help you craft another marketing plan. But it can help you build a business foundation that relies on strategy and product planning.

A shaky foundation makes a shaky structure. A strong foundation makes a durable home. A home that won't blow over whenever some wolf shows up with a huff and a puff.

If you're absolutely certain your business model, product line and brand are perfectly positioned for world domination and all you need is the right marketing, this is not the book for you.

If you think you could use some help creating a better business model and crafting products that sell themselves, this book may help.

CAN YOU TRUST ME?

For what it's worth, my background includes a Bachelor of Business Administration in Marketing from a top 50 business school, 1/3 of an MBA and 25+ years in branding, marketing and business consulting.

I opened my Etsy shop in 2008 as a side gig that grew steadily. In 2010, I quit my day job (as a brand strategist) and reached 40,000 sales and a substantial revenue on Etsy alone.

Over the years, I collected ideas and philosophies that shaped the shop and its achievements. I built my shop on these concepts, most of which I haven't seen mentioned elsewhere.

I held most of these ideas close to the chest. So close that I'm uncomfortable sharing them now. It feels scandalous and risky. Are they too valuable to be shared? What if it destroys my own shop?

Then I said, "Why not?" My use of Etsy is changing anyhow. I decided to put these secrets on paper to pay it forward as others have done for me.

Some ideas may seem brilliant to you yet absurd to someone else. Some may resonate now, others a year from now.

Can you trust me? I hope so. If you read this book with an open mind, taking notes along the way. In the end, I hope you'll trust yourself to make smart business decisions going forward.

HOW THIS BOOK IS ORGANIZED

This book aims to help you build a foundation that grows your business, revenue and happiness.

The book starts with business basics, moves to strategy and brand, then grazes over pricing. Somewhere in there is product planning, which is where I think many Etsy shops miss the mark.

SEO (Search Engine Optimization) secrets follow product development. There's so much conflicting information about SEO. I'll try to sift through the chaos to help you master it for your shop.

After that, you'll find listing strategies and shop management tips followed by a brief marketing interlude and some customer service secrets.

The book ends with a special section called "Your Notebook". You'll find questions to help you think differently about how to build your business.

Each tip is brief and to the point, with around 100 words each. I decided if I needed more words, you deserved another tip.

HOW TO USE THIS BOOK

I hope you'll keep this book, read it and refer to it whenever you need a little inspiration. I hope it expands your idea of what your business can be.

I also hope it gives you confidence in your abilities, not frustration with all there is to learn.

LET'S GET STARTED.

SET-TING UP SHOP

This chapter assumes you read Etsy's guides and understand SEO, Etsy Ads and how to set up your shop. Intended to augment (not replace) what you already know, it offers a few "getting started" ideas even Etsy veterans may find useful.

These ideas aren't secrets, but important things to consider as you open a business.

READ ETSY'S SHOP GUIDES. EVERY WORD.

Read and absorb everything Etsy says about running a shop on Etsy. They're the true experts on themselves. You can find information in the help pages, on social media, in their podcasts and more. Also, subscribe to their newsletters, follow their (multiple) social media accounts and generally become a crazed Etsy stalker. Understanding how Etsy thinks and what they value can help you thrive on Etsy.

FORM AN OFFICIAL BUSINESS ENTITY

In the USA (and beyond), forming a legal entity (sole proprietorship, limited liability company, etc.) legitimizes your business and provides protection for personal assets should you encounter injuries, lawsuits or unforeseen problems. The IRS likes it, too. Check with your legal advisor or do your own research on requirements and options for your location (city, county, state, country) and product type (some are prohibited, others require special labeling, etc.) so you're organized and protected appropriately.

GET BUSINESS CHECKING AND CREDIT ACCOUNTS

Managing your finances is much easier if you separate business and personal expenses. Etsy's finance system had a glitch in 2019 and those paying fees with personal debit cards were over-drafted. Yikes! Get a business-only checking account to minimize this kind of problem. While you're at it, pay your Etsy fees with a credit card so surprises don't compromise your food and housing funds. Credit cards also offer quick and easy credit should you need it for raw materials and supplies.

USE ETSY AS A MARKETPLACE NOT AS AN ONLINE SHOP

The primary benefit of selling on Etsy is its status as a marketplace filled with shoppers ready to buy things. Treating yours as an independent shop may demand more money and effort than it's worth in revenue and reward. Etsy can be an expensive and frustrating endeavor for those unwilling to take full advantage of its existing market, features and global recognition. While you'll have to obey their rules and roll with their frequent changes, the low cost of entry and active shoppers make it worthwhile.

DIVERSIFY IF YOU WANT TO QUIT YOUR DAY JOB

If you want your business to be your sole source of income, expand beyond Etsy. Even if your Etsy shop is profitable now, it can crash at any time due to market shifts and hiccups you never imagined. Diversify by creating your own site, listing on other marketplaces, teaching, writing, doing craft fairs, offering wholesale, etc. Etsy can be a fickle partner. The more you spread your talents around, the better you can keep a roof over your head. For additional ideas about quitting your day job, see how to build a nest egg on page 51.

FOLLOW SMALL BUSINESS MASTERS

If you only seek information on Etsy tips & tricks, you'll miss out on opportunities and ideas hiding inside other business content. I follow *Forbes*, *Entrepreneur*, *Success*, *Wired* and *Inc.* for everyday ideas and inspiration. I watch *Shark Tank* and *The Profit*. *The Wall Street Journal* may also spark a few ideas. These resources can help you think more strategically. While we're not all going to build craft empires, we can all carve a rewarding career by expanding our idea of what's possible. These publications will help.

DON'T EXPECT SALES FOR MONTHS

Starting an Etsy shop is always exciting. You're filled with hope that someone, somewhere wants your stuff. Still, months can go by before you get more than a few visits or a single sale. It may take longer if you're new to selling online, photography and running a business. While you wait, learn. Tweak your shop until your photos, presentation and offer are better than everyone else's. Master SEO (see page 60) and collect feedback from other sellers. Be patient, but actively seek information to help you get that first sale.

STRAT-EGY & BRAND

A goal-focused strategy combined with an authentic, values-driven brand can position your shop for long-term success.

This chapter shows you how to incorporate marketing concepts in your master plan now, so you can focus less on marketing later.

This chapter forms the foundation of everything you learn in this book.

DEFINE YOUR VALUES EVEN IF IT SEEMS RIDICULOUS

Defining 5-10 personal and professional values may feel like corporate claptrap, but it's the foundation of an authentic brand. The process can focus your product line, policies and marketing plans while connecting you more deeply with prospective customers. Search on-line for "define your values" and review articles that ask tough questions. Questions will get to the root of what's driving you, a list of words won't. As you ponder your core values, identify who you are, not who you think the market wants you to be.

CREATE A VALUES-BASED BRAND NOT A CARICATURE

Your brand isn't just a banner and logo, but a perception created by experiences people have with your business. It's formed by artwork, policies, packaging, social media and everything you do that the buying public can witness. Build your business and its brand around your values (see page 25). This helps create a memorable, genuine experience for shoppers and customers alike. Avoid crafting a false caricature of your business just to get sales. Authentic brands deliver far more growth and durability.

BE BRAND-CONSISTENT THROUGHOUT THE BUSINESS

Create policies, packaging, pricing and a presentation that matches your brand and values. For instance, if your products are high-priced and high design, offer free returns and stylish packaging. If you value environmentalism, use "green" shipping companies and donate a portion of sales to an eco-friendly charity. Find ways to express your values-driven brand throughout the business, not just in its presentation. This creates an authentic, durable identity to connect your business more deeply with its target market.

WRITE A BUSINESS PLAN EVEN IF IT MAKES YOU UGLY CRY

Creating a simple road map of where you are, where you want to go and how you plan to get there can be the difference between a hobby shop and profitable, fulfilling business. Even if you can only squeeze out a single page, include values, goals, a schedule and a budget. Add market and competitive analyses if you can bear it. Your plan doesn't have to be complicated or set in stone and it can ensure squirrel-chasing doesn't compromise your mission. Review your plan regularly, at least once per year.

ESTABLISH AN ONGOING SWOT ANALYSIS

Almost as old as marketing itself, a SWOT (Strengths, Weaknesses, Opportunities and Threats) Analysis can help you understand how to position your business and every product in it. I use my running SWOT Analysis to develop new product lines, rethink my brand and explore random ideas. I augment it every time I discover something worth noting, such as "professional packaging" under strengths and "e-cards" under potential threats. Include anything, however fleeting, that can help or harm your business.

DEFINE MULTIPLE TARGET MARKETS

Women between 30 and 80 may buy your products, but something unites buyers besides age and gender. Define those details by demographics, lifestyle, traits, habits, hobbies and more. It might help to build a profile of your "perfect customer". There may be multiple market niches, depending on your brand and product line. There's an article on my website about target markets, along with tons of resources on-line and beyond. Making un-researched assumptions about your market can severely limit your growth.

UNDER PROMISE AND OVER DELIVER

We all know that person who constantly gloats but fails to deliver reliable results. Don't be the shop that oversells only to disappoint paying customers. As you craft your brand and presentation, keep a few small perks in your pocket. For instance, if all orders include a free gift, don't promote it. Customers may mention it when they leave feedback, or not. Use the same strategy with product benefits. Keeping a few minor perks close to the chest may help customers love you more and remain loyal to your brand long term.

PROD-
UCT
PLAN

Your products can anchor your company more than anything else.

This chapter will help you discover what the market wants from you and how to use your unique set of skills to give it to them.

You'll learn to turn a product you love into a product the market loves. Then you can build a profitable shop that thrives.

SELL WHAT PEOPLE WANT — NOT JUST WHAT YOU LIKE

Selling regularly means offering a product people want. Not one your mom loves. Not one your friends said you should sell. Not one you think is brilliant. You can reach a huge, diverse market on Etsy, but if your mix of product, positioning, price and promotion isn't something the Etsy market wants, you won't thrive. Figuring out what the market wants requires research, an understanding of your unique skill set and the ability to spot market gaps that you alone can fill.

BUILD PRODUCT LINES, NOT RANDOM PRODUCTS

Offering full product lines may improve revenue, visibility and search placement (see page 67). Launch at least three products per line with a similar theme (same style, product type, etc.). Build new product lines around successful products or augment popular lines. Flytrap's "bad parking notes" were wildly popular so I offered printables with exceptional results. You can also augment popular product lines to appeal to diverse needs, such as different genders, ages, features, uses, functions and so much more.

FIND MARKET GAPS AND FILL THEM WITH YOUR STUFF

Build your business when you decide, "I can do that **better**." Not just "I can do that." Don't do what's been done. Do it better, faster, cheaper, with more features, more options, better packaging, a better design, a complementary product, different materials, a different interpretation, etc.. Solve old problems in new ways. Improve on existing products. Understand what needs aren't being met and fill them with a fresh business model, product, style or collection. Thrive as an innovator, not as a copycat.

AVOID VIOLATING ANYONE'S IP

As you develop products, don't copy anyone else's. Not only can this lead to issues like lawsuits, fines and a closed Etsy shop, but it's also no way to build a sustainable business. Research IP (Intellectual Property) laws around the world. If your product is inspired by something else, make sure yours cannot be confused with the original by anyone anywhere. Avoid using commercial names, characters and quotes even if "everyone is doing it". Let your creativity drive your business, not someone else's.

UNDERSTAND THE PRODUCT LIFE CYCLE

Most products have life cycles. They emerge, grow, stabilize then decline. It's important to understand where your products fall. I use this rule of thumb: If the growth rate declines (sales are up 120% one year and 80% the next), that product is in decline. A revenue decline almost inevitably follows. At that stage, it's critical to rework the product, find new markets or develop something new to replace it. Awareness of product life cycles can be the difference between a lifetime business and a fleeting blip.

USE GOOGLE TRENDS TO ASSESS VIABILITY

Google Trends can help you assess general interest for your product ideas. Search for a keyword or phrase then filter results by the maximum amount of time (2004-present). If the trend is growing, you might be able to take a piece of the pie by resolving an unfulfilled need. If it's declining, you might be able to capture a die-hard niche with a clever feature or presentation. Both can make compelling strategies. The trend data will help you refine the product, keyword strategies and market niches.

SEARCH FOR PRODUCTS BEFORE MAKING THEM

Before you develop or decide to sell a product, always ask: "Does anyone sell it already? Can I make it better?" Assess the marketplace by searching for the product on-line and in brick & mortar stores. Scan product reviews and social media of everything you find. Understand what currently exists and how it's being sold. This helps you decide whether or not to offer the product at all. If your idea isn't sufficiently unique and in demand, you may need to make some big adjustments or abandon the idea altogether.

SELL KEYWORD-REPEATABLE INVENTORY

Offer some products and lines that are repeatable and scalable (sellable by the thousands as with cards, printables, etc.). This may improve your feedback volume, search placement and ongoing revenue stream. More products with similar keywords may elevate all products using those keywords. So the more you offer, the better off you may be. You'll learn more about this in the "SEO & Keywords" chapter. Selling OOAK (one-of-a-kind) products is fine, but a shop full of OOAK listings may struggle on and off Etsy.

PLAN YOUR MARKETING BEFORE SELLING STUFF

Before you invest time, money and energy on a product idea, figure out how to sell it. This may include investigating keywords, scanning social media, researching advertising, scoping out the competition and more. If you don't know how you'll move the product beforehand, you may spend time and money trying sell a product you can't even give away. Understand how to position it, market it and sell it before you build it or invest in it. It will save you some headaches (and maybe a little crying) later.

USE ETSY'S SEARCH BAR TO DEFINE PRODUCTS

The Etsy search bar auto-complete feature helps shoppers find what they want. It can also help sellers determine what products to create. Just type any word or phrase into the search bar and note the phrases that appear below it. Create or acquire products that fit those keywords better than anything you see in search results. I think it's one of the best ways to develop product ideas. Choose products based on currently used, reasonably popular keywords that fit all the other criteria mentioned in this book.

IMPROVE ON POPULAR ETSY SHOPS AND PRODUCTS

If search results for any keyword deliver over 3,000 listings and a few best sellers on the first page, it's probably a popular search phrase. Try to improve on those bestsellers in style, features, presentation, etc.. If you can't improve on them, keep targeting different words until your listings can be among the best options available in search results. While it doesn't pay to copy popular products (see page 36), solving unmet needs with your product and listing can help you outsell the bestsellers in time.

VERIFY BESTSELLER POPULARITY BY REVIEWS

Some products earn Etsy's "bestseller" badge because the listing sells more often than others in a particular search. This doesn't necessarily mean the product is popular. If you want to determine "bestseller" popularity, look at customer reviews under the "bestseller" listing. If all reviews are for other products from that seller, it may not be a bestseller yet. It might indicate the product is new or growing. If you want to improve on that product, recognize its popularity may not be what it seems.

USE OTHERS' REVIEWS TO SELECT PRODUCTS

If a competitive product dominates in search results, you may still be able to improve upon it. Look over customer reviews for the listing to see what customers complain about. Solve those problems with your product. For example, if customers complain about slow shipping or bad service, commit to next-day shipping and elite service. Flytrap customers complain about the product size. Anyone who wants to create a larger version (without copying mine, see page 36) has an opportunity worth exploring.

CONSIDER PRODUCT LINES BY PRICE POINT

As you group products into product lines, consider dividing your lines by price point. Think: affordable, mid-range and exclusive. You can remove unnecessary features on affordable products and add options and customization to exclusive lines. This ensures your products accommodate various budget perspectives, shopping styles and buyer needs. It's a simple way to group products into lines that may also improve your SEO and income strategy, as explained on page 55.

COVER EVERY SEASON WITH YOUR PRODUCT LINE

Etsy is popular for seasonal gifting. Offer products specifically for every big shopping season, such as Valentine's Day, Mother's Day and Back to School. Do the same for life events including retirement, birthdays and new babies. You can even create products for things like "National Hamburger Day" and "Squirrel Appreciation Day" (legit holidays). This can help you enjoy year-round sales and keyword domination. Especially on gifting occasions for which nobody else makes an appropriate product.

BE CRITICAL OF YOUR PRODUCTS EVEN IF IT HURTS

As you explore keywords, critically assess how your products measure up. If every product on the first three pages is better than yours, target different keywords. How do you know what's better? Answer the question, "Why is your product better than the competition?" with benefits or features that only you can claim. If you can't do it, your product may not be better. In addition, if search results include many products with better photos and features, you may struggle to compete. Be confident, but be self-critical as well.

IT TAKES MANY GOOD DEEDS TO BUILD A GOOD REPUTATION, AND ONLY ONE BAD ONE TO LOSE IT.

BENJAMIN FRANKLIN

PRICING & MONEY

I'm no expert on money. My philosophy demands protecting yourself from disaster while maximizing revenue. You'll discover techniques for achieving both of these in the following chapter.

Some of these ideas may seem insane, but if you want to sustain your business long term and / or quit that day job, they can help.

BUILD A HUGE NEST EGG TO QUIT YOUR DAY JOB

Quitting your day job requires planning and fortitude. If that's your goal, keep your real job until you save at least 12 months of living expenses. If you own a home, shoot for 24 months. This ensures you can cover expenses during slow periods, handle home maintenance needs and feed yourself while you build your business. You should also be prepared to pay up to 50% of all profits toward taxes. These guidelines may seem discouraging, but they will help you make smarter business decisions with confidence.

CONSIDER BASING PRICES ON DEMAND AND REVENUE

Products sometimes move faster at lower prices so it might be worthwhile to consider a demand-driven pricing strategy. For instance, if you can move 1,000 units ever year at $10 for $10k annually or 500 units at $15 for $7.5k annually, it might make sense to set a price of $10 to maximize annual revenue rather than profit per unit. If you use this method, make sure you cover production, marketing and tax costs. Also, make sure you can produce enough units to meet higher demand levels.

LOWBALL NEW PRODUCT PRICES

Consider setting the introductory price of any new product 30-50% lower than the competition. Because products that sell more frequently may get priority placement, such a strategy may help you achieve search domination, especially if the product moves at the lower price. You can gradually raise the price if you need to slow demand or maximize profitability. I'm willing to lose money in the short term to achieve search domination long term. But beware: sometimes higher priced items move more quickly on Etsy.

ADD VALUE WHEN YOU WANT TO RAISE PRICES

If you're not making enough money to justify the effort of your business, consider adding value to raise prices. For example, offer free returns and charge an additional 10% per unit. Or use high-style packaging, elite photography and a sophisticated presentation and add 30% to the price. Value-added opportunities include elite service, extra features, more options and customization. It's a great way to raise prices or position your company as a luxury business without adding much to production costs.

OFFER SEVERAL LOW-PRICED LISTINGS

Many products under $10 sell quickly and often. Since products that sell regularly seem to get priority search placement, all products can be elevated by fast-moving options. Use your top keywords list (see page 68) to define affordable products and help you dominate in critical searches. Even if yours is a luxury brand, a few cheap options on Etsy can aid placement and growth. Lower priced items may include accessories, attachments, ornaments or any in-demand product you can make quickly and easily.

INCLUDE MARKETING COSTS IN THE PRICE

Some marketing is inevitable for every business. Marketplace selling fees, web hosting fees, etc. are part of my marketing budget. Etsy Advertising can play a key role as well. I recommend sellers pay no more than 20% of the cost of a sale (10-15% is better) for marketing and fees, unless specifically seeking high search placement for a keyword. So, if you offer a $50 item, raise the price by up to 20% (or to $60) to cover your marketing costs per sale. It simplifies costs and enables more freedom with your marketing dollars.

CONSIDER MANAGING RISK WITH SELF-INSURANCE

Self-insurance enables shop owners to cover some financial risks rather than paying outside insurers. Especially if your products are inexpensive or ship for under $10, self-insurance may be cheaper and enable you to respond better to customer problems. It may seem scary, but it's easy to manage. Just determine what percentage of orders encounter problems (damages, returns, lost, etc.) each year. Then add that percentage to the price of each product. If 5% of orders run into problems, add 5% to prices.

PAY THOSE STINKING TAXES EVEN WITHOUT A 1099

My dad always said, "Don't f*ck with the mafia or the IRS." I tend to overdo it with the IRS, giving them more money than they're owed. Even if you don't want to be a lunatic like me, report your income from your Etsy shop whether or not you get a 1099. Pay your state, city and county taxes while you're at it. It may save you headaches down the road, such as being audited and owing a fortune in back taxes when your company booms.

I FIND THAT THE HARDER I WORK, THE MORE LUCK I SEEM TO HAVE.

THOMAS JEFFERSON

SEO & KEY- WORDS

SEO (Search Engine Optimization) means your stuff shows up in search results for the right customers at the right time.

There is so much conflicting information out there about SEO on Etsy. Even from Etsy itself!

In this chapter, I'll try to help you sift through the chaos and craft your own secret formula.

READ EVERYTHING ETSY WRITES ABOUT SEO

Etsy has an entire section of their website devoted to "getting found". Read it, absorb it, learn it, then read it again. Reread it every six months, since it changes all the time. All the experts in the world cannot compete with what Etsy says about how Etsy works. Even if experts claim to know better, they don't. Etsy knows Etsy. Start there.

DON'T BELIEVE SEO IDEAS UNTIL YOU TEST THEM

Many Etsy experts claim to know exactly how you can master SEO. They'll lure you in with glitter and kittens while promising a lifetime supply of chocolate. Even if everyone says some guru is an infallible SEO genius, those experts know nothing about your shop, its analytics, the competition or anything else that defines your best SEO strategy. Even as you read this chapter, sit next to a giant vat of salt to enjoy it with. There are many great ideas out there. Collect them. But test them before you commit (see page 103).

REMEMBER: NO TWO SHOPS ARE ALIKE

Navigating SEO can be as confusing as the US Tax Code. This guru says one thing, that guru says another and you're left screaming and crying into that pink satin crocheted pillow your grandma made. True story. The only truth about Etsy SEO is that SEO guidelines vary by product, shop, category and more. Which means it's exponentially variant. Your shop is not like that shop. You are special and unique. Test every SEO "truth" you learn (see page 103). Yes, I said that twice. That's how important it is.

OPTIMIZE YOUR SHOP FOR ETSY, NOT SEARCH ENGINES

Etsy is a marketplace, offering a niched group of shoppers ready to buy stuff. This is its top benefit for shop owners. Catering your Etsy SEO to outside search engines may interfere with this perk. Optimize your SEO specifically for Etsy while trying not to piss off outside search engines. For example, don't keyword stuff titles (a major search engine no-no) unless it benefits your unique Etsy shop and use Etsy (not Google tools) to research Etsy keywords. If you'd rather focus on outside search engines, build your own site.

REMEMBER: SALES LEAD TO BETTER SEARCH PLACEMENT

This is the single most important thing to remember about SEO on Etsy. Any listing that sells seems to get priority placement, making it easier to get more sales that improve placement further and sales and... you get it. So always focus on whatever keywords generate the most sales. If a keyword perfectly describes your item and nobody buys it when they search using that word, you're using the wrong keyword. Focus on keywords that sell your products, not just on words that accurately describe them.

BE BETTER THAN YOUR KEYWORD COMPETITION

One of the hardest tasks to master is comparing your shop to the competition. It requires a finely-tuned self-critical eye (see page 48) that doesn't devolve into despair when everyone else is better. Your photos, product details, policies and offer need to be at least as strong as everything on page one of search results for your target keywords. If you don't measure up, improve your product, presentation and offer or find a different search to target. It's the most important SEO strategy that nobody ever seems to talk about.

BECOME A SUBJECT MATTER EXPERT TO DOMINATE

One trick I use is repeating keywords in multiple product listings. Some say you shouldn't "compete with yourself", but that's nonsense. While you don't want to repeat them too often in the same listing (outside of regular copy), repeating them shop-wide can position you on Etsy and search engines as a Subject Matter Expert (SME) for those keywords. All listings using those words may get a placement boost. It's my biggest secret that SEO people often get wrong. But don't take my word for it. Test it (see page 103).

DEFINE 5-10 TOP SHOP KEYWORDS

Most shops can select a few top shop keywords that define what they are. Two of mine are "funny" and "paper". Create a list of 5-10 words that represent your overarching shop concepts, your target market, your style, etc.. Use these words throughout your listings, shop, marketing materials and social media hashtags -- basically whenever you write copy for your shop. This reinforces your brand in shoppers' minds and may aid search placement. It also helps you capitalize on the SME theory (see page 67).

DEFINE 10-25 KEYWORDS FOR EVERY PRODUCT LINE

Select 10-25 keywords for every product line that capture its essence, style and attitude. You can use style words like "modern", recipients like "mom", holidays like "Easter" and so forth. It might help to match these words to Etsy's predefined attributes, though I haven't tested this myself. Include a few of these keywords on every listing in the group. Name a shop section with the most effective of those words as well. This can help you become a SME (see page 67), which may be a back door to search domination.

DEFINE 50-100 KEYWORDS FOR EVERY PRODUCT

Define 50-100 keywords — per product — to test. "Pardon me, but did she say 100 keywords **per product**?" Yes, I did. This forces you to try tons of keyword ideas for every product until you can find a combo that actually drives sales. Sales are the goal. Not your idea of accuracy. Even if you think a keyword or phrase is perfect, you don't get to decide that. The market decides. So test 50-100 keywords, discarding those that don't actually drive actual sales. Then test 50-100 more until you find the right mix.

DON'T JUST DESCRIBE THE PRODUCT

Sure, you want to include keywords that describe the product ("cat hat"). You can also test words that represent what the product may be to someone. Such as recipient, season, occasion, material, dimension (small, huge), color, price range (under $10), style (modern, Victorian), gender, age range (teenager), relationship (husband, mom), etc.. I'll say it again: You don't decide what makes a great keyword. The market does. They do it by buying your products when you use the right keywords. Remember that.

USE THE ALPHABET TO FIND POPULAR KEYWORDS

I'm about to share one of my biggest secrets. Most people know the Etsy search bar auto-completes with popular phrases. I always add a space plus one letter to any word or phrase to find additional keywords. Search "birthday gift for a" for one list and "birthday gift for b" for another. You can even search "birthday gift for ab", ac, ad, etc. Use the alphabet to find additional keywords. Etsy search also highlights similar phrases at the top and bottom of searches. Test every relevant highlight you find (see page 103).

TARGET SEARCHES WITH BESTSELLERS

Etsy bestsellers get more sales than other products in search results. If no bestsellers appear in search results, that keyword or phrase may not be popular. If there are three or more dissimilar bestsellers in search results (as you find with "unique"), the bestseller might be popular when paired with other words. Searches with bestsellers indicate peak popularity and a worthwhile growth opportunity. If your product, presentation or offer is better than the bestsellers' in search results, that's an excellent keyword to target.

TARGET WORDS WITH 3,000+ SEARCH RESULTS

Unless you have an extremely niched and high demand shop or a just-for-fun shop (and proved it by testing), target searches with more than 3,000 results. Test smaller searches to see if you can capture unmet needs ("unicorn hat adult" is a small key phrase with potential). But don't over-commit to them. Small searches often mean nobody uses that phrase. Unless there are relevant bestsellers in search results, consider choosing different keywords. As always, don't follow me blindly. Test it to be sure (see page 103).

UNDERSTAND WHAT CLUMPING MEANS

Clumping means search results show multiple listings from a single shop "clumped" together on one page. Clumping may indicate bestselling listings for that keyword alone or when paired with other keywords. When you see clumping, add words to the target phrase. For instance, if "gold jewelry" delivers clumped search results, change your search to "modern gold jewelry for women." This shrinks the number of search results (shoot for under 100,000) and enables you to find your piece of the selling pie.

USE TOP KEYWORDS IN YOUR SHOP SECTIONS

Using keywords in your shop sections can improve search placement on outside search engines (and maybe Etsy). Name sections after product group keywords (see page 69). For instance, Instead of calling a section "Earrings", add a descriptor like "Baby Earrings" or "Drop Earrings". The more target keyword instances in your shop, the higher you can place in search results. In addition, don't use extra spaces (e a r r i n g s) or add characters. Search engines won't read those section names if they're not literal.

USE SHOP KEYWORDS AS PART OF NATURAL COPY

Include top shop keywords (see page 76) in Titles, About, Policies, FAQs, Updates, Shop Members, Sections, Announcements and Product Details. Search engines (maybe not Etsy) use these sections to help determine search placement. Use those keywords as part of readable, conversational copy – not tossed in as a jumble of unrelated words. Remember what I said about not pissing off search engines (see page 64)? This is an easy way to capture off-Etsy traffic without compromising your Etsy SEO.

TEST GENERIC KEYWORDS ALONGSIDE NARROW ONES

People who search generic terms like gift and bracelet are different from those who search with more depth. Shoppers often won't find what they want with a broad search, so they'll narrow it down with filters and additional keywords. Include broad keywords in your titles, but only in tandem with more specific ones. For instance, include "pillow" along with "purple teenage girl's bedroom". Be sure to check where your products fall when various filters are used, like attributes, free shipping, sale and pricing levels.

TEST TO FIND THE RIGHT TITLE FOR EACH PRODUCT

Product titles are one of the most important factors that determines search placement on and off Etsy. The strength of your titles will vary by keyword, product, shop, competition and more. Adopt whatever title strategy generates the most favorites and sales – since sales matter most (see page 65). Test long and short titles (see page 103). Test repeating and single-use keywords. Carefully test to understand what works for your shop without blindly adopting every suggestion you see.

REMEMBER THE POWER OF KEYWORD COMBOS

The phrase that gets the sale isn't your exact product title or tag, but some combination of the words you use in both places. Look for clues about what works in your Etsy stats and analytics. You'll probably see a few similar phrases bunched up toward the top of the list and some peculiar stragglers toward the end. Because it's hard to know what search phrases shoppers use to make a purchase, combining the most relevant, if seemingly random, keywords may deliver the best results.

THE CREDIT
BELONGS TO
THE MAN WHO IS
ACTUALLY IN THE
ARENA; WHOSE
FACE IS MARRED
WITH DUST AND
SWEAT; WHO
STRIVES VALIANTLY,
WHO ERRS AND
MAY FALL AGAIN
AND AGAIN,
BECAUSE THERE
IS NO EFFORT
WITHOUT ERROR
OR SHORTCOMING.

THEODORE ROOSEVELT

PROD-
UCT
LISTINGS

This chapter explains how to craft product details that encourage shoppers to buy from you. Getting it right requires an intimate understanding of your product, your market and the competition.

I'll show you how to build trust and desire while removing sales barriers. Your listings can prove to shoppers that your product is the best option available.

UNDERSTAND HOW ONLINE SHOPPERS SHOP

Shopping starts with a need. Maybe someone needs a gift for mom, a decor item or a solution to a problem. Shoppers see tons of options when searching. They click on photos and prices they like to narrow the options. Then they compare those options and buy whatever best meets multiple needs (price, features, etc.). You need to outshine the competition at each individual point — lead photo, price, description, supplemental photos, policies and shop details — in the shopper's process.

REMEMBER: PHOTOS GET THE CLICK

I'll say it again, with feeling. Combined with price and perceived value, your photos narrow shoppers' options from thousands of choices in search results. Your photos should a) stand out from others in your most relevant searches and b) appeal to your market more than everything else shoppers see. Be different in a good way without trying to close the deal from the photo alone. The object is to catch the right shopper's eye without making them cringe – so your photo wins the click instead of someone else's.

MAKE YOUR LEAD PHOTO DIFFERENT AND UNIQUE

The lead photo is the first photo in your product listings. It's also the photo shoppers see in search results. If your photo looks like everyone else's, it may be impossible to get noticed. Help your photos stand out through staging, angle and/or styling. If everyone else shoots on a white background, shoot on gray. If everyone else leads with an in-use shot, lead with a close up. Understand why certain listings in search results attract your attention. The right lead photos may get the click... and the sale.

ADD LEAD PHOTO BADGES TO SOME LISTINGS

Adding graphics or badges to lead photos that spotlight something important to shoppers can help your product get the click. Try adding a badge for key benefits like "fast shipping" and "top seller". During the holidays, add "Arrives by December 24th". If everyone in your category uses badges (I'm looking at you, printables), you may want to avoid it. Use badges to differentiate your photos, not to copy everyone else. Craft a consistent badge design and test various styles to learn what works best.

DOUBLE ETSY'S PHOTO SIZE SUGGESTION

For 2019, Etsy recommends photos over 2,000 pixels wide. I use photos that are 3,000 pixels wide and set the resolution to 150 ppi (pixels per inch), when 72 is standard. This ensures photo clarity for those using high resolution monitors and devices. Device resolutions consistently improve and Etsy updates their size recommendation regularly. Staying ahead of it means you don't have to update all of your photos every time Etsy updates their guidelines. It's a handy time-saver for busy, large shops.

INCLUDE DIVERSE PHOTOS IN EVERY LISTING

Etsy allows shops ten photos per product. Use every slot. Include a close up shot, a shot of the product in use, a dimension shot and a policies shot for returns and shipping. Take photos from all angles of the product, including the bottom and back. It might help to show creative uses for your product. I include a shot of my packaging, expedited shipping options and related products. Be creative in your use of every photo slot. Remember: Photos should help you close more deals, not protect you from rare problems.

TRULY SELL PRODUCTS WITH PHOTOS AND DETAILS

The object of descriptions is to convert shoppers into buyers. Use photos to sell your product as if there are no words. Use words to sell your product as if there are no photos. Show shoppers why your product is better than everything else they've considered. Focus on product benefits ("You'll be flooded with compliments when wearing this necklace!") over features ("It's 18" long with a polymer clay giraffe pendant.") to evoke an emotional connection to you, your product and your shop.

MAKE IT EASY FOR SHOPPERS TO BUY FROM YOU

If photos get the click, your product details help seal the deal. Always include the following in your descriptions: Dimensions (metric and imperial, including height, length, depth and weight), cleaning and care, allergens, eco-friendly notes, packaging and shipping information, your return policy, etc. Make it easy to purchase immediately without looking around your shop, contacting you and waiting for a response or shopping elsewhere because they couldn't get the information they needed from you fast enough.

DON'T INVENT SALES BARRIERS IN YOUR LISTINGS

It may be tempting to use listing details protect yourself, such as "I am not responsible for lost packages." But I think that's a mistake. Your descriptions are about converting shoppers into buyers. Don't make demands on your customers just to give the most basic level of service most e-tailers offer. While you're at it, find creative ways to avoid barriers, such as using variations or expanding your return policy. Your demands might protect you. More often, they give shoppers a reason to take their money elsewhere.

INCLUDE KEY INFORMATION IN MULTIPLE PLACES

Redundancy with important details helps both you and shoppers. Because we all absorb information differently, add key information in Policies, FAQs, product listings, banner, badges (see page 86), announcements and shop updates. This makes it more difficult for customers to miss critical information and minimizes issues later. For instance, if you offer free returns or have unusual terms customers must follow, multiple references to these facts can improve conversions and protect you at the same time.

OPTIMIZE DESCRIPTION FORMATS FOR ALL DEVICES

Etsy shoppers purchase using desktops, tablets and smartphones, each of which uses a different screen size. It's more important to have scannable details than short ones. Group information with capitalized headlines (DETAILS, POLICIES, etc.) with one-line bulleted details under each headline for quick scanning. When needed, use paragraphs separated by a double line. Verify that your descriptions are easy to scan and read on various device browsers and Etsy apps. Avoid weird line breaks and bad formatting.

SLOWLY TWEAK YOUR PHOTOS, LISTINGS AND SHOP

Never transform your whole shop (photos, titles, tags and descriptions) at the same time unless it's grossly under-performing. You might accidentally change that one magical thing that was driving all your business. Instead, make changes a few listings at a time. Wait at least a few weeks (preferably a few months) to review your data and determine whether or not the change improves your business. Adopt changes that show measurable growth over time, not just those you like. It's okay to go slow if that means you get it right.

SHALLOW MEN BELIEVE IN LUCK. STRONG MEN BELIEVE IN CAUSE AND EFFECT.

RALPH WALDO EMERSON

SHOP DETAILS

Shop details like Policies and FAQs can reinforce your brand and improve your SEO on and off-Etsy.

This chapter will show you how to take control of your shop and build trust with your market using Etsy tools, while optimizing your operations and policies.

COMPLETE ALL ETSY SHOP SECTIONS

Etsy has many shop sections, including a banner, announcement, About, FAQs and Policies. As you build your shop, complete every section available. This may aid search placement and certainly reinforces your brand. Plus, the more you complete your shop, the more trust you build with customers. Use those top shop keywords (see page 68) and craft a united look and feel for all copy, graphics and photography. Cohesion is a key trait of a successful brand. Unifying your shop sections is a good (and simple) first step.

USE POLICIES TO GENERATE SALES

Many use policies to protect themselves from rare issues with customers. I see them as an opportunity to build trust and move more product. Instead of creating policies around what happens when a package is lost (a rare occurrence), say you'll take care of your customers regardless of what happens. Staying flexible in your policies helps build customer trust and allows you to deal with issues on a case-by-case basis. Add a new policy only if you run into ongoing problems, not for a one-time incident.

SAY "YES" TO EVERYTHING— AND CHARGE A PREMIUM

Instead of saying "no" to something customers want, charge a premium for things you don't want to do. If customers want overnight shipping but you don't want to rush to the post office, charge a "rush" fee. If you generate more sales just by offering more shipping options, it's worth it. The same goes for any service-forward shop feature, like custom orders or free returns. You know what I hate? Custom orders. So I set a $300 minimum. That's the price that makes me say, "Well, okay. You talked me into it."

ALLOW CUSTOMERS TO RETURN AND CANCEL

Because shoppers can't touch your products, allowing returns is compulsory; even for custom products. A generous return policy makes it easier to convert shoppers into buyers. In addition, if an order hasn't shipped, there's no reason to deny cancellations. Until returns or cancellations become a problem in your shop, allow them. If you're concerned about losing money on custom orders, establish a non-refundable deposit system so shoppers pay for raw materials prior your acquisition of them.

TEST EVERY NEW ETSY FEATURE WHEN IT'S RELEASED

Dozens, maybe hundreds, of things drive search placement. Each feature Etsy adds is designed to grow revenue for Etsy and its shops. Those who adopt Etsy features like "free shipping over $35" and the oversized banners they introduced a few years ago may see improved search placement. Test each feature for a few months (not just a few days), trying various strategies until you find a formula that works for you. Don't give up on any feature just because you don't like it. Let the numbers decide for you.

ADOPT NEW FEATURES, BUT DON'T EXPECT MIRACLES

Readily adopting new Etsy features may help with search placement and your success. But remember: If you don't already have consistent sales, adopting new features won't deliver them. Focus more on offering products people want, presenting them effectively and creating the best offer. Once you master that, everything else will get easier. Adopting features is a bonus to grease the wheels, but it will never be the wheel itself.

TEST EVERY CHANGE BEFORE YOU COMMIT

Adapting features, keywords and even product design can all be tested on Etsy. Copy any listing and change one thing: a feature, the price, the photos, etc.. Watch both listings for a few months (not a few days). Then count visits, favorites and sales to determine which performed better. It's critical to change just one thing so you know what made the difference. Plus, a few hundred visits to the listing gives you more reliable results. It's not foolproof, but it's one of the best ways to learn what works and what doesn't.

INCLUDE TIME FRAMES IN SHIPPING PROFILES

If you don't use calculated shipping, include time frame estimates in your shipping profiles. Pad the time frames by 20% and make sure you deliver on the promise at least 98% of the time. This can improve conversions and enable customers to make a quick decision. Worry less about rare deliveries outside the time frame (and subsequent bad feedback) and more closing the sale. The sale is the goal. You can manage customer service issues later (see page 120), if there are any.

WATCH YOUR VISITS TO FAVORITES RATIO

Favorites can indicate general interest in your product. Especially when a product is new or doesn't sell, favorites may reveal if your keywords, price or listing details need work. Lots of favorites and few sales imply a problem with the listing or shop itself, since the lead photo got the click or favorite. Few favorites and many sales suggest a well-positioned product since shoppers buy rather than save it for later. Products with a visits / favorites ratio under 10% may need a great deal more research and adjustment.

WATCH YOUR CONVERSION RATE OR VISITS TO SALES RATIO

Your conversion rate or visits / sales ratio is a great way to track demand shifts for each product. Conversion rates below 1% suggest an under-performing product, presentation or keyword strategy. Products with low visits and a high conversion rate (over 10%) may suggest an exceptional keyword strategy or a highly niched product. Industry standards recommend a conversion rate over 3%. As you review yours, give it some time – at least a few months – before concluding anything is awry. Data takes time.

RECOGNIZE WHEN DEMAND SHIFTS

As I mentioned on page 37, I believe products are in decline when growth declines, which precedes a sales decline. By the time sales decline, your shop could be cooked. Use Etsy's data download and create (or purchase) a spreadsheet to help you track sales. There may also be external data analysis apps to explore. Track products, product groups and your overall shop. Review stats weekly and analyze them monthly. This will keep you abreast of shifts so you aren't blindsided by a sudden death.

ACT FAST WHEN DEMAND SHIFTS

When you notice a demand shift, make sure it's not part of your normal seasonal trends. It takes a few years to understand seasons for any shop. Cope with changing demand by expanding your marketing strategies, adding distribution methods and / or re-imagining the product. Be sure to check your keyword competition for any new entrants in your space. You may just need to make a few adjustments. Quick action can keep food on the table as you develop new products and lines to replace the dying ones.

TRY TO AVOID PUTTING YOUR SHOP ON VACATION

Etsy offers "vacation mode" when you need to shut down for any reason. Unless you're facing an emergency, I recommend extending your processing times rather than putting the shop on vacation. Because sales beget placement, shutting the shop down for any period means other shops get the sales you don't, thereby prioritizing their products over yours in search results. While extending processing times may also impact placement, it doesn't seem to have as much negative effect as "Vacation Mode."

TACKLE SLOW PERIODS WITH RENEWING AND SALES

Whenever sales seem to slump (or post-vacation), renew 5-10% of items every day until you're back on track. Renewing listings may offer a slight and temporary placement boost for a minimal cost. You can also run a flash sale, offering a discount for a few days or weeks, which is useful for shoppers who select the "on sale" filter. I've used both methods successfully when sales declined. These simple and affordable tricks can keep dying products afloat while you select new products or expand your distribution.

SEEK OVER 100 REVIEWS ANNUALLY

Reviews are critical to a shop's success. Because Etsy's review score only counts the last 12 months of reviews, getting at least 100 every year prevents one unhappy customer from crushing your feedback score. This may require you to sell 500 units annually, since customers don't always leave reviews. To get more reviews, you can offer printables, inexpensive items or add ons under $10. Offering more opportunities for reviews can give you a nice buffer for those situations you cannot resolve amicably.

REVIEW AND ANALYZE YOUR SHOP DATA REGULARLY

Etsy stats and analytics are a treasure trove of information. Keep your eyes on the numbers or hire someone to do it. You can discover what products are growing versus declining just by comparing last year's data to this year's. You can discover why sales slowed or exploded by looking for shifts in keyword popularity and your traffic source. It's a great way to understand what's working and what isn't in your shop. It can also help you avoid being blindsided by unexpected shifts.

TAKE PERSONAL CONTROL OF YOUR SHOP

When your shop struggles, don't commiserate with others, "hope" things change or blame Etsy or the economy. Use that energy to form an action plan and take control of your business. While outside forces can contribute to tough times, you're the only one who can do anything about your shop. Take direct action to overcome whatever obstacle you face. It's fine to vent or complain for a minute, but if it becomes a weekly (or more frequent) habit, it's a problem that will certainly interfere with your success.

MAR-KETING & ADS

Though this still isn't a marketing book, I had to share a few ideas.

Primarily, focus on what comes easily, not on what some guru says is important. People thrive when they're having fun, not when they're struggling to correct "flaws".

Use these ideas to help launch your shop into the world.

FOCUS YOUR ENERGY ON WHATEVER IS EASY FOR YOU

I believe we are good at things that are easy or interesting to us. If you love social media, devote yourself to mastering it for your business. If Facebook ads are fun and easy for you, invest in them. While it pays to explore every available marketing option, those who can't figure out Instagram or become homicidal just thinking about Google Ads should dump or outsource those tools. Promotional opportunities that interest you become personal marketing sweet spots worth exploring.

TEST ETSY ADVERTISING LIKE YOUR LIFE DEPENDS ON IT

Etsy's advertising system won't work for everyone, but make sure you test it extensively (see page 103). Mastering Etsy advertising may improve both search placement and sales. Consider it an investment in your future. Maximize your budget while testing, even if you lose money initially. Experiment by advertising different products, using different keywords and adjusting your budget periodically. Continue advertising any product that generates sales and tweak it until you're satisfied with results.

INVEST BIG ON ETSY ADS FOR NEW PRODUCTS

Your success with Etsy ads will vary by product, search and shop (just like SEO). When you launch a new product or product line, invest time and money to find a formula that sometimes (if not always) lands your new product's ad on the first page of search results. Ads are most effective when your keywords are on point. If your ads don't result in sales, adjust your keywords until you find the right strategy. Continue to invest time and money in ads until sales take off (or you just oh-my-god can't anymore).

MASTER PHOTOS BEFORE MARKETING

Photos can make or break your shop. You don't need a fancy camera to shoot well, but you do need to understand basic photography principles. Great photos combine correct lighting with appealing styling. Study the photos of top-selling shops and learn all you can about styling and product-specific photography. Unless you have a groundbreaking product, any marketing is a waste without top-notch photos. Perfect photography before approaching influencers or publications that can put you on the map.

BE ON SOCIAL MEDIA FOR SHOP CREDIBILITY

Many people despise social media, saying "I don't care what people from high school are doing!" Still, social media lends credibility and may aid off-Etsy search placement. Create accounts for Instagram, Facebook and at least one other platform. You can automate your posts across social media accounts while reaping the rewards. Even posting every few months is enough to keep your social media accounts functioning, legitimizing your business and offering a search engine placement boost.

CUS-TOMER SERVICE

The secrets in this chapter will help you handle customer issues with confidence and grace, even in the wake of Etsy's Order Dissatisfaction Rate (ODR) launched in 2019.

These ideas can prevent rash decisions that compromise your values, integrity and future revenue.

CLOSE THE SALE OVER PANTY-BUNCHING

When customers ask for something you can't or don't want to do (like give them a discount), state what you can or will do rather than turn customers away. For instance, if a customer haggles on price and you want to throat punch them, don't say, "My prices are firm." Instead, invite them to follow you on social media for sales and special offer alerts. If shoppers want a bulk discount, don't say, "No". Say, "Yes. Orders over $35 get free shipping." Don't get upset over special requests. Get opportunistic. Find a way to say "yes".

FOCUS ON YOUR SERVICE LEVEL MORE THAN REVIEWS

Reviews are important. But making decisions based on bad-review fears may leave you anxious and compromise your service level. For example, even if you issue a refund without a return, customers can still leave a bad review. Instead, be exceedingly polite, generous and over-communicative – especially when delivering bad news or dealing with difficult customers and situations. Let your values (see page 25) guide you instead of fear. It's good for your attitude, brand and Order Dissatisfaction Rate.

BUT GO OVER-THE-TOP FOR THOSE FIRST 100 REVIEWS

Etsy's review score averages reviews from the last twelve months. Bend over backwards and to the left for those first 100 reviews every year. Why? Because if you have ten 5-star reviews and one 1-star, your feedback score is 90% (and looks like 4.5 stars). But if you don't get a bad review until the 101st, your score will be 99% (and looks like 5 stars). It's probably worth it to lose a few bucks with one unhappy customer if you gain five others who purchase because they appreciate that near-flawless score.

VALUE WARM AND FUZZY EXTRA WORDS OVER BREVITY

People often try to be straightforward with customers, but being less blunt helps people feel all warm and fuzzy about you and your shop. Even if you prefer getting to the point, over-communication softens bad news and ensures you cover all the bases (which can save some headaches later). Consider, "I don't offer bulk discounts." vs "I'm so sorry. I don't offer bulk discounts. But I am having a sale in two weeks so be sure to check back. Thank you!" The former feels dismissive, the latter feels friendly and trustworthy.

PAUSE BEFORE RESPONDING TO REVIEWS OR OPEN CASES

It always pays to calm down before dealing with difficult customers. If you're upset for any reason, give yourself up to 24 hours to gain composure. You can vent to friends (but never on social media) or scream loudly from a hilltop. Remember, every interaction impacts your brand. If you respond when agitated, you may not be professional or effective and you might compromise future business. When you respond, be extremely kind and patient. Especially if you have fewer than 100 reviews (see page 123).

RESPOND TO BAD REVIEWS LIKE A PRO

Review responses should be written for future customers, who don't care about your excuses. Customers care how they'll be treated. There's a popular article on my website about responding to bad reviews – read it. If you decide to respond publicly, don't blame the customer. Limit your response to 60 words and use the communication sandwich: Apologize, briefly address the issue, offer a resolution and apologize again. This shows future customers you care about your service level more than you care about your ego.

DON'T PANIC WHEN SOMEONE OPENS A CASE

Cases can seem scary. Like your boss (Etsy) is staring over your shoulder telling you what an idiot you are. But they're not such a big deal, especially if your service level is top notch. Customers may open a case because they don't know how else to contact you. Be extremely polite and move all communication to the case itself, documenting anything relevant. Open cases may impact your search placement, but unless they comprise more than 1% of sales, they shouldn't be a deal-breaker for your shop. Keep calm and breathe it out.

OPTIMIZE QUALITY, SERVICE AND SHIPPING

Shoppers can select customer feedback that mentions quality, customer service and shipping. Keep all three at the top of their game for every customer so reviews for all three stay positive. Any poor review that mentions one of these should receive additional attention. Try to resolve the issue outside of the review system, withholding any response until you hear from the customer. Be generous in your resolution negotiation and encourage unhappy customers to change their reviews if it seems appropriate.

IT IS A PAINFUL
THING TO
LOOK AT
YOUR OWN
TROUBLE
AND KNOW
THAT YOU
YOURSELF
AND NO ONE
ELSE HAS
MADE IT.

SOPHOCLES

YOUR NOTE-BOOK

The next few pages include questions to help you think differently about how to build a better business on and off Etsy.

Treat it like your diary, jotting down answers freely and without fear of judgment.

Review this section regularly. If you lose your spark, these notes might help you bring it back.

What five things, ideals and (dare I say it?) values
are most important to you and this business?

_____

_____

_____

_____

_____

What big dreams do you have for your shop?

_____

_____

_____

_____

_____

What is your most absurd annual revenue dream?

_____

How many employees, if any, do you want?

_____

Where do you want to be at this time next year?
How about in five years?

_____

_____

_____

_____

_____

List at least five revenue generation strategies
you can use like teaching, writing, wholesale, etc.

_____

_____

_____

What do you hope the market and world at large
says about you and your business?

_____

_____

_____

Which business leaders do you admire most?

_____

_____

_____

In what television show(s) would you love your
products to be featured?

_____

_____

_____

In what publication(s) would you love for you or
your products to be featured?

_____

_____

_____

What retailer(s) would you love to stock your products?

_____

_____

What product(s) would you love offer one day?

_____

_____

List your top strengths as a person, an Etsy shop owner and a business.

_____

_____

_____

_____

_____

What things do you not do as well as others who sell products like yours?

_____

_____

_____

What features or options do you think people want that they don't get in products like yours?

_____

_____

_____

What kinds of things might get in the way of your success? For instance, your family, attitude or technology.

_____

_____

_____

_____

_____

Describe the type of customer you hope will become a super-fan of your shop and products.

_____

_____

_____

What are three of your ideal customer's top hobbies or recreational activities?

_____

_____

_____

What are your top customer's favorite television shows, movies, musicians, etc?

_____

_____

_____

_____

_____

List at least 5 words that describe your shop.

_____

_____

Pick one of your products and list at least 50
words that could describe it.

What policies and strategies can you create to
reinforce your brand?

_____

_____

_____

_____

_____

What visuals can you use to connect more deeply with like-minded shoppers, including photography staging, styling, filters and more?

_____

_____

_____

_____

What messaging or copy style feels most effective for your personality and shop? Should you be funny, serious, quirky or something else?

_____

_____

_____

_____

Brainstorm some creative ways to make it easy for customers to order from you.

_____

_____

_____

_____

Check out a few competitors on Etsy, Amazon and elsewhere. What do they do better than you?

_____

_____

_____

What do you do better than your competition?

_____

_____

_____

What marketing ideas seem interesting to you?

_____

_____

_____

_____

What ad campaign types (print, web, etc.) are most appealing to you, personally?

_____

_____

_____

Think about the best customer service you ever received. What made it memorable?

_____

_____

_____

What unique or creative customer service practices would you like to adopt for your shop?

_____

_____

_____

What clever things can you do with your packaging to make your shop memorable?

_____

_____

_____

_____

What do you want customers to say about your business?

_____

_____

_____

How can you retain customers for repeat business?

_____

_____

_____

How will you stay motivated if or when business declines?

_____

_____

_____

How will you celebrate achieving your goals?

_____

_____

_____

one.

Your business, loyalty and

Printed in Great Britain
by Amazon